Identity Theft

Reclaiming Your Victory

D1569887

Antoinette J Bey

CANNONPUBLISHING

May you [...] and Reclaim your victory! [signature]

Identity Theft

Reclaiming Your Victory

Antoinette J Bey

CANNON**PUBLISHING**

Cannon Publishing

P.O. Box 29176

Charlotte, NC 28229

Phone: 888-502-2228

Website: www.cannonpublishing.net

Printed in the United States of America, North Carolina.

Printed in the United States of America.

ISBN #: 9798416092252

If you desire to order copies in bulk, please contact Antoinette Bey at: ann@mrsannbey.com.

Dedication

This book is dedicated to the individuals from my past who spoke against me, belittled me, used, abused, and turned their backs on me. THANK YOU because without you executing your roles so well in my life, I wouldn't be the strong, courageous, and amazing sister, mother, aunt, cousin, wife, & Woman of God I am today.

I also dedicate this body of work to my mother Lizjo (*insider*) and all the other women (and men) who have been afraid to live in their truth due to fear of being judged, talked about, and ostracized by their peers. No one battling through a spiritual identity crisis should have to do it alone and because I have let go of the fear of what others may think to share my personal journey to recovering my identity, you can now work toward gaining strength and courage to do the same.

By the time you finish reading this book, you will be able to recognize signs of an identity crisis and have workable tools to overcome them so that you can begin to live a life of authentic freedom, as well as walk into and receive all God has created you to be.

Acknowledgements

I would like to acknowledge my husband Quentin because he is my number one fan and supporter. I appreciate you for loving me through the hardest times even when I failed to express my true emotions.

To my personal coach and mentor, The Trailblazer, Carla R. Cannon-Lawrence, for paving the way for women to blaze their own trails and live in their authentic truths.

To Betty Fudge Fisher for the spark—Queen continue to "BeU" always.

I acknowledge my sister Laurn Colley Valentine for being my confidant and cheerleader when I wanted to throw in the towel, and for always reminding me of who I am.

I would like to give special acknowledgements to my spiritual covering, Pastor Jay, and Marilyn Haynes. I thank you two so much for trusting me and always providing support and encouragement as well as for always being available to assist whenever and however you can.

Lastly, I acknowledge all six of my birth children and the bloodlines that follow and I pray that this written work provides a footprint for you all to follow so that you may always walk in your truth as well as remain free from any attacks of identity theft that may come against you or your households. I love you all more than words can express.

Table of Contents

Foreword 1

Introduction 3

Chapter 1: Not My Idea 9

Chapter 2: Innocence Gone.. 17

Chapter 3: Robbed of Self-Awareness 27

Chapter 4: A Little Girl's Secret 34

Chapter 5: Mental Poverty 42

Chapter 6: Releasing the Victim Spirit.......................... 51

Chapter 7: Disbelief + Doubt = Unbelief 57

Chapter 8: My Pain Paved the Way 63

Conclusion.. 69

Resources 72

About the Author.. 101

Foreword

Identity Theft is a resource that I believe is timeless and can be passed down from generation to generation. In a loving yet unapologetic manner, Antoinette opens her heart and allows us into her journey of what life has been like for her.

As you read the pages of this book, I encourage you to remove any thoughts of what you expect it to be and do for you. Trust me, it is so much more and will be a reference guide throughout your life.

I've had the opportunity to spend time with Antoinette over the years due to my relationship with her daughter, TeLeah, as well as her becoming a client. She is not the type of person who is going to sugarcoat her feelings or tell you what you want to hear.

So often, we reject what we do not understand rather than taking the time to step into the shoes of someone else's life and at least try to understand why they are the way they are, and what life has been like for them.

I invite you to do the same with Identity Theft. Whether you have experienced the same things or not, trust me, someone you know has or is currently or if you keep living you may have similar experiences.

This resource is a guide on how to persevere against all odds and commit to becoming who you are destined to be. Whatever you feel has been lost, know that God is a redeemer and what *was* will never outweigh or outshine what *is* to come.

Get ready for the ride of your life and be sure to share with a friend when you're done, so we all can break free together!

Carla R. Cannon-Lawrence
"The Trailblazer"
www.CarlaCannon.com

Introduction

I decided to write this book for several reasons. The first was to kick fear in the butt. I come to serve notice that I am who God says I am and no longer will I allow fear of what others may say about me to prevent me from reaching my full potential in Christ.

The second reason is to serve a notice of correction to Satan that his whisper of lies that he had me believing all these years about being selfish, crazy, a poor wife and mother, unwanted, and worthless were all lies from the pit of hell.

Finally, I want my life and the challenges I've overcame to be a beacon of light to someone who may be attempting to find their spiritual identity through life's struggles. I want others to know that their current condition does not determine their final destination.

You may be reading this and like me, have experienced challenges in your life that derived from being robbed of your spiritual identity. I know too well what this feels like. I also know what it looks like because that is where I was up until October 2017.

Spiritual locksmiths were used in the form of one-on-one sessions with my coach and mentor Carla R

Cannon, personal therapy with a licensed therapist, and reading books. Eventually a lock was picked that allowed me to share my story unapologetically and authentically. I stand in my truth to prayerfully assist you, as you read along, and utilize the tools within to pick your spiritual lock as well.

I want you to know that you are not reading another book from someone trying to walk you through a process they have never experienced. In my life I have survived and thrived through many things but only by God's grace and mercy.

At the age of six, I became my mother's caregiver. Between ages four and eleven, I was being sexually molested by a family friend. By sixteen, I was pregnant and forced to have an abortion. By twenty, I was a single-mother and by thirty, I was in my second marriage. By the time I reached forty years old, I was ready to throw in the towel because everything I spiritually, mentally, and intellectually understood about life had all been challenged and I was beginning to believe that perhaps there was some validity in what I had been labeled.

Selfish, crazy, a poor wife and mother, unwanted, and worthless seemed to fit me very well according to my circumstances.

Two things kept me going: Thinking about who would care for my children in my absence and knowing that no one would love them the way I would. I also did not want to leave them feeling abandoned as I had felt when my mother attempted to take her own life.

The other thing was that on the day of my mother's incident, as a little girl, I made a promise to myself that I would never allow anything in life to make me so sad that I would try and take my own life.

By the time I turned forty-four, I did my best to view life from a different lens and as a result, things began to shift in my favor. I started to feel more at ease about whether I was going to survive this thing called life. A series of events transpired and I felt certain that things were going to be okay.

'But how?' you may ask. Well, grab your favorite beverage and a snack because I'm going to take you back to how it all began and walk you through to where I am now, so you've got to hang in there with me until the last page!

Now, I would be lying if I told you I clapped my hands three times, turned around and yelled WHOOP, there it is, and my life began to transform. It would even be stretching the truth if I didn't tell you about the countless nights, I stayed up scolding God about the cruel and unfair life He'd given me and questioning Him repeatedly about the broken promise I recalled from Him in 1996.

I had been robbed of my spiritual identity and for years, could not figure out how to restore it. To make bad worse, Satan was always there to torment and remind me of just how little I must have meant to anyone in life because absolutely no one ever asked me questions about how I was coping with the grief associated with my mother's failed suicide attempt.

No one ever asked me how I was doing genuinely. I received counseling as a kid (per my mother's suggestion) but apparently the counselor did not see any abnormal characteristics that warranted continued support. Shame on them because the little girl inside was certainly wounded.

After turning forty, there was a point in my life where I experienced difficulty coping and I would question God's existence. But, did you know that God will not allow you to become overly consumed with the issues of life that your heart turns completely away from Him? Let me remind you that God has plans for us and being lost is not one of them. When the pressure is on, and He sees His children becoming consumed with what is going on in their lives, He will reach down and pull you out of whatever it is you are going through and allow you to begin to restore your identity in Him.

The objective of sharing the process to my victory is to provide hope and healing to anyone experiencing an identity crisis. I am letting go of the fear that I have operated in for so many years.

For a long time, I believed the story of my life was insignificant because it was simply supposed to be that way. I felt like my voice would not be heard and the fear of feeling as if no one cared to hear about my journey, prevent me from sharing my story with others.

When I decided to share, I became overwhelmed with not knowing where to begin so I told myself, you have gotten this far in life holding on to your pain, so let it go and live life. The important thing is to know you can let go and live life by leaving the weight and baggage behind, but never neglect an opportunity to help someone else overcome. Afterall, my pain serves a purpose which has ignited a desire within me to help others experience an internal awareness that will direct them to change their lives for the better!

My overall hindrance was shame, embarrassment, and denial of the things that happened to me growing up. I believed that if I told myself and others that I was alright, and life was alright, then everything was alright. Well, it wasn't, but it is now!

I've learned over the years that if your testimony helps *one* person, you've impacted a nation already. I invite you now, on a journey to join me in breaking free from spiritual identity theft by taking the time out after reading each chapter of the book and meditate on situations that have robbed you of being able to experience wholeness in every area of your life.

I also invite you to journal your feelings along the way and at the end of the book, be sure to take full advantage of the resource I am including just for you which is my 7-Day Personal Discovery Journal.

The exercises in the journal are designed to serve as a guide for you to begin the journey to reclaiming your personal identity so that you can walk out the life God originally had planned for you. So, what are you waiting for?

Let's begin the work!

Chapter 1

Not My Idea

It was January 2018 I had no idea what I wanted to do or where I wanted to go in life, but I knew for sure that there was something more in life that I should have been doing. I was hopeful in everyone's life around me. I was able to cheer others on through their storms although a tsunami was happening in my life. I was lost, alone, and miserable until that day I had an epiphany to quit my job. I was not prepared to quit at all, but the outlandish thought was what led my wheels churning to start a quest to find out what more life had in store for me.

The journey stemmed from a conversation I had with my boss. I was dissatisfied with my position as a Home Manager in a mental health facility that housed twenty of the most physically aggressive men within the Southwest Michigan region. Although I did not have a sharp vision at the time, there was a burning desire for me to do more with my life. Let me take you back to that day. It is something about the beginning of a new year because it was on January 16, 2017. I was sitting in my office chair when I looked up at my boss and said out of nowhere, *"By this time next year, I'm gonna be a half millionaire"*. He responded after a brief pause with *"So you gonna start playing the lottery?" "No,"* I said, *"I'm gonna follow my dream".*

I had no idea what the dream was, and I certainly did not know what following it was supposed to look like. What I was sure of was that I did not want to work ten to twelve hours a day for someone else making them richer while I lived in agony knowing there was more in life that I was purposed to do.

If you read my previous story, *"The Weapon Was Formed, But It Didn't Prosper"* in Volume Four of *Down for the Count: Bouncing back From Life's Blows*, you remember I shared my story of feeling as if my life purpose was to care for my mentally ill mother. I thought it was my purpose because that part of my journey began at a very young age and continued through a large part of my young adulthood.

My mother was not fully able to provide the most stable of child rearing but when she was at her best, she did an amazing job with what she had the ability to do. I cannot say that all my childhood was completely bad because there were some advantages to my experience as being my mother's caregiver.

As a result of not having much stable parent support, I learned at an early age how to be resilient as well as responsible. There were times when it was jokingly stated, "*Yes I'm the mother but, she actually raised me.*" As a young adult, a spirit of pride rose within me that made me feel the joke was okay, yet I also harnessed a bit of anger inside. I convinced myself for that statement to be made, it showed that even as a little girl, I was intellectually capable of tasks beyond my years when in actuality, the hand I had been dealt in life robbed me of my childhood.

The road to discovering my spiritual identity, realizing that Satan had come to rob me while I was in my mother's womb, and the road to rebuild that identity has not been an easy one. By the time you read this book, I will have endured hardships, disappointments, discontentment, rejection, and despair. I will have quit embarking upon my journey a thousand times and a thousand times I will have started over because I refuse to not allow the hell I have gone through, to not serve the purpose of a greater good for my children and their children's children as well as the women and men out there who have experienced or will experience a spiritual identity crisis.

My life wasn't the ideal life I would've chosen for myself but eventually I came to realize that all the things I experienced were a part of God's plan to help others along the way. As I write at this very moment and reflect on the past, I am in awe of how I can construct, plan, and execute the way I do considering my past and can I tell you once more; NONE of this has been a part of my plan, I mean NONE. I would not be crazy enough to build a life centered around a little girl wounded and lost in the middle of a battlefield with all sorts of land mines going off, while she is trying to navigate her way back to a place of safety. That would certainly fit the definition of insanity!

Here is a funny but true story that sheds light on how lies can create unconscious beliefs and negatively impact an individual. Prior to growing old enough to realize my brother had been lying to me, I believed that my mother had found me in a cabbage patch and feeling sorry for me, decided to bring me home. I know what you are thinking, well that was cruel of him. RIGHT, my sentiments too, LOL!

Older siblings can be so mean and do not get me wrong when I say that. My brother has never done or said anything maliciously to hurt me. As a matter of fact, He was always very protective of me and would have gone to jail in a New York minute had he believed anyone else was trying to hurt me.

Anyway, let me finish the story. I recalled as a little girl riding in the back seat of the car whenever my dad was taking us on country drives, thinking to myself and wondering if my brother was just making fun of me, or was I really retrieved from a cabbage patch. I would stare out of the window in hopes that we would drive past this cabbage patch that my mother had found me in, and I would once and for all be able to identify my home.

Living in the house with my mother, brother, and my dad whenever my parents were not split up, made me feel alienated because as it was, my childhood was never normal. I was the child of an unwed mother who had hooked up with a married man and conceived an undesired pregnancy.

If Satan had had his way, I would not be here as those were not the most favorable conditions to bring a child into the world. I must admit, when I look back now, I am appreciative that my mother did not take the easy road out and abort me; however, the enemy was not finished with his antics.

Remember I used the description 'undesired pregnancy'? There are circumstances that open the door for the spirit of rejection and abandonment to enter in. YES, you read that correctly. A child can in fact experience abandonment and rejection through the mother's womb!

So, as I was explaining, none of what I was experiencing at the time of entering this journey to rebuilding my spiritual identity was easy and all my previous relationships were used to define who I was as a person. By now, my resume' tells tales of a woman with a scarred childhood, two failed marriages, being molested as a child, and doing my best to be a better mother than I had been given an example of; yet knowing my best was not good enough for my children but that was my best at the time.

The one thing I knew for sure was that there was a plan for my life and that was an inner feeling I could not shake. Satan's lies started to become much louder until they screamed the words, "abandoned," "rejected," "worthless," and "undesired."

There came a point when I felt everything about my life was proving that Satan was right and the hope inside of me was either false, or I was being robbed by a force greater than I, and I had no knowledge of it or was too weak to fight back.

The urgency I felt inside of me that day in the office of my previous job was so strong that I came home from work one night and told my husband that I was going to put in my two-week notice. Luckily, the Lord was listening just like Satan was listening. My husband placed his hand on my back and gently said, *"Babe, I don't know if this is right or not, but I just feel like there is more that God wants you to do at your job before you leave.”*

I cringed inside hearing this but I believe in the Word of God. The scripture tells us that obedience is better than sacrifice, therefore, I stayed at the job a while longer. It was a little over a year later and although that was not my idea, I patiently waited until God allowed me to leave at the completion of my assignment.

Before I go any further, I want to ask you a question. Do you have a yearning inside of you to do something such as begin a new career, start your own business, or become a homeowner?

Take a moment to write down the thoughts you have that might keep you up at night or make you drift off into a daydream.

Chapter 2

Innocence Gone

I had not given much thought to my life as it relates to dealing with traumatic events until I was well into my forties. I understood that past experiences shape who we become in our later years, but because in so many ways I thought I was *fine,* I never looked at my past as a fault or point of reference as to why I was the way I was or had any influence on my decision-making skills at the time.

I considered my past, at times, to be a plus for me because of the wisdom, and intellect it took to deal with the issues surrounding my mom. I also felt I had a life that stood to be desired because I had freedom that many of my peers did not have.

I had seen so many of the young women around me appear as weak and void of inner strength to live life aside from having relationships that defined their happiness. What I later discovered was that I had a misconception of this thing called Queening.

In 2007 an altar worker at church after praying for me asked if I had been molested to which I replied, "No." Fast forward to 2010, I had begun seeing a counselor because I felt that now at forty, my life was in crisis mode, my marriage was about to kill me, and I needed answers immediately.

During a session, my therapist asked me if I had ever been molested, to which I replied "No." We went on with the session and I left to return home and during that drive I received a revelation of what had happened to me as a little girl. Approaching a flashing yellow light, I saw flashes of me being in a dark room as a little girl. I could vaguely remember this room but recalled being taken into the room numerous times.

It is amazing what God will reveal to you when you are mature enough to handle the truth. I was now able to say aloud, *"I was molested."* Super excited for the revelation, I rushed home and ran into the bedroom to deliver the news to my husband.

While I stood there rambling in excitement of the revelation, this was his first time ever hearing about me being molested. He met me with a blank stare, but I continued with the conversation about the alter worker at church and then being asked by my counselor about being molested but having no recollection at the time of questioning.

During the moment of my sharing, he never asked me questions or showed any care or concern about what I was telling him. It was almost as if he wasn't listening.

I started thinking, *"How can my husband be so cold and blasé about something this sensitive in nature?"* I began to feel ashamed and embarrassed for being excited for my revelation, so I discontinued the conversation and walked away.

I cannot pinpoint how far or how long the years of molestation occurred or if this were the only person who violated me as a little girl, but I could safely say it transpired between approximately four and six years old. I'm realizing not only did I forget the molestation, but I also stuffed the trauma of seeing my mother attempt suicide in my presence.

God has a way of putting a shield of protection around our minds so that the things that are meant to destroy us will not overtake us. He knew I could only handle dealing with Satan taking one gift but not two of the most important gifts of a little girl's life: her mother and her innocence.

My innocence was taken away from me and my life would forever be shaped by the occurrence of things that happened to me during this time and the years to come.

I had never spoken openly about being molested and was able to stuff the memories so far to the back of my mind I could not recall the incidents. It brings truth to the saying, out of sight out of mind. I could now acknowledge what happened to me and I also knew that it was not my fault.

I made up my mind that I did not have to be angry or bitter about what had happened to me back then. Now let me be clear about trauma. Trauma doesn't always result from sexual molestation. A person can be traumatized by verbal, physical, or psychological abuse as well as witnessing tragic events such as I did. Trauma can happen at any stage in life, but I am referring specifically to the trauma I experienced.

If you are reading and you are triggered personally about some type of trauma that you endured at any stage in your life, stop and journal about it now then come back and finish reading.

If you are okay and can go on, let's continue as I will give you another opportunity to journal after this chapter.

Trauma is defined as an emotional response to a specific event such as abuse, an accident, or even natural disasters. People have a natural tendency to deal with trauma either positively or negatively. People will either go on in life and use their traumatic experiences to help others or they will indulge in negative behaviors or activities to help cope.

Studies have found 45-66% of the adolescent population struggled with the use of substances experiencing traumatic events in their lives (*Making the Connection, p. 2*).

Through research, it was also determined that teens who had experienced physical or sexual abuse were three times more likely to battle with substance abuse. Of the 70% surveyed, who received substance abuse treatment, they abused substances in response to trauma exposure.

Basically, that means that trauma can affect one directly or indirectly. You can be the one who suffers the trauma or simply be exposed to trauma such as witnessing a loved one attempt suicide, seeing a tragic accident, or seeing someone die. I pray that you are not one of those statistics but if you are, I want you to know that you can become a victor of your circumstance.

If you are a victim of physical or sexual abuse, I really want you to take away from this that trauma is not always your fault. Some trauma was caused, and it was beyond your control and those things you don't have to accept responsibility for; however, you are the only responsible party that must be willing to do the work to rebuild your personal identity.

If you were a little child, you would not be responsible for how a friend, or stranger mishandled you. You are only accountable to the little girl or little boy inside of you who was wounded due to that person's sickness.

I also want you to know that your trauma does not have to be your reason for remaining broken. When Satan attempts to rob you of your spiritual identity, he will stop at nothing to try and make you feel as if the things that happened to you are your fault, or that no one will believe the things that you say have happened to you.

He will even make you feel ashamed and embarrassed about the things that happened to you. I know this to be true because I experienced many mixed emotions about being molested. I felt guilt at one time for "allowing it to happen;" whatever that meant.

Remember the part of the story where I shared with my husband about being molested and how he seemed to have not been paying attention. Well, he may not have been, but Satan brought it back to his recollection one day during a heated conversation.

It was during the conversation he began saying hurtful things about me being crazy and telling me no one would want to be with me if I didn't stay with him etc. He eventually told me that it was because I had to give myself away for someone to want me, that was the reason I was molested.

The words did not come out that way verbatim, but it was the gist of what he was telling me regarding being molested. This was a lie of Satan. Another antic of his to keep me blinded and unaware of my spiritual identity being stolen from me.

Let me assure you that neither myself, nor you for that matter, if that be your witness, are exempt from Satan using the same trick to steal your identity. Remember what Tamar experienced when she was raped by her brother Amnon in the Bible? He was in love with her until he took what he wanted.

He discovered that lust and love are not the same. After he raped her, he called for his friend to put her out and lock the door behind her (see 2 Samuel 13: 1-19). Has that ever happened to you when a guy (or girl, because women do it to men also) pretended to be in love until after the sexual encounter, then they ghost you?

This my friend is also another avenue Satan uses to rob you of your identity. It confirms feelings of being unwanted, unloved, undesired, and unworthy. If you are the perpetrator of this kind of behavior, it may be a confirmation or warning that there is a fear of commitment due to having abandonment and rejection issues and you may want to seek therapy to find a healthy resolution.

Listen, if things have felt out of sort for you, and you desire, to live a life of mental harmony and peace, it will require having the ability to reconstruct your spiritual identity, but it will also necessitate that you be totally honest with yourself and your inner child, and then be willing to openly admit that you were violated.

Whenever we hear about things that resonate with us based on our own experiences, it has a way of triggering uncomfortable emotions inside of us.

(If you or someone you know are struggling with mental health, substance, or alcohol use and would like to speak with someone go to samhsa.gov or call 1-800-662-HELP (4357))

Were there emotions that were triggered in you as you were reading my story? I want you to reflect over your life and use the lines below as an opportunity to write about an experience that happened in your past (or something that may be currently happening) that may have traumatized you.

_____

_____

_____

_____

_____

_____

_____

_____

_____

_____

_____

_____

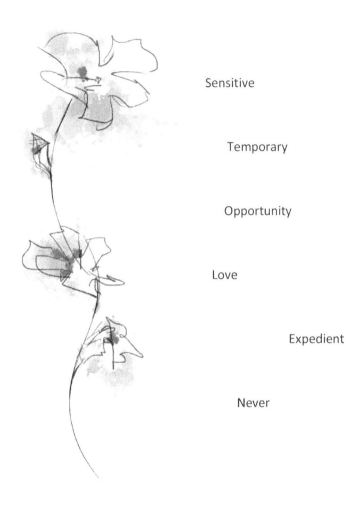

Sensitive

Temporary

Opportunity

Love

Expedient

Never

Chapter 3

Robbed of Self-Awareness

Self-awareness is necessary for building and developing healthy relationships. Without having a sense of self-awareness, you are prone to being in relationships with people who treat you however they desire.

The problem with that is although the individual may not be mishandling you intentionally, because one's self-awareness resulted from their identity crisis, they wound up getting hurt by others because they don't know how to ask, or demand being treated a specific way and they typically end up walking away feeling like they are inadequate for the type of relationships/friendships they deserve or desire and low self-esteem creeps in.

When a person is robbed of self-awareness, it can also leave them vulnerable to connecting to people who have ill intentions towards others. Once again, the one void of self-awareness ends up getting used by these kinds of people as they are crafty in their approach, yet their prey is simply an easy catch.

Self-awareness is a part of your spiritual identity; therefore, it is important that you understand who you belong to and not only know, but also learn to value your self-worth. However, when robbed of this knowledge, your quest, as was mine, is to obtain the keys to build up that skillset and with determination my friend, it is most certainly doable.

To begin the work in this area, you might want to look more into participating in some cognitive restructuring lessons which consists of changing your negative thought processes and replacing them with positive ones.

Cognitive restructuring therapy teaches you how to gain an understanding of moods and feelings that are counterproductive to living free from stress, anxiety, and other negative thought patterns. If you look around you, as you learn more about this, you will begin to see how predominately many of us operate with stinking thinking.

At an early age, Satan had been successful in ruining my self-awareness by using the people closest to me, and those whom I trusted most. The robbery began with sexual molestation from a family friend and was later proceeded with two of my closest friends who would also take sexual advantage of me.

Looking back I realize their manipulation was used as a tactic of Satan to have me believe that this was the identification of love and respect of family and friends, therefore, it could not be all bad. Throughout my formative years my brain wasn't comprehending or processing exactly what happened or what was going on.

Most children who suffer any sexual abuse tend to exhibit negative behaviors but as I recall, my behaviors did not show up until later in my teenage and early adult years.

To my knowledge no one knew about my inner struggles other than the person whom I believed to have been my best friend, because we shared a similar experience in life.

However, I eventually came to find out they were using my weakness to their advantage by further taking advantage of me through sexual acts. As an adult, I can see how I learned early in life to allow people to treat me in whatever way they chose too.

Somewhere deep down inside of me there was an internal rage and deeper in the core of my being, there was a mini tsunami beginning to take life inside this small frame of a body.

As much as this loving and caring individual tried to come out, there was a bitter person that was always sitting on the couch in my mind. This was the individual who would drive me to think what they wanted me to think about how I viewed myself, and how others viewed me.

Satan tethered with my mind and made me feel as if I had to get others before they got me. I had to leave them before they left me, I had to stop being friends before they quit being friends with me. Even after reaching primary education, I would still have people who would coerce me into sexual acts, and I thought that's how friendships worked; after all this was learned behavior at an early age so it must have been right. It had to be okay.

The enemy had robbed me of my self-awareness. He had stolen my life from me –at least that was his plan. But I want you to know that God will take what was stolen and use those very things to promote you to your next level.

How, you ask? By equipping you with the necessary tools and sending you to take back what Satan had stolen.

Silence the enemy and the voices he has sent as a distraction to prevent you from hearing the voice of God speaking to you through your circumstance. Turn up the voice of God by committing to daily prayer and meditating on His word.

Temporary stress, strain, disappointment, heartaches, and such happen when we neglect to see the enemy at work in our lives, or we neglect to learn about ourselves to gain understanding of why things are out of sorts. Determine the cause of these temporary issues and then develop a plan of action to overcome them.

Opportunity presents itself daily to shower you with brand new mercies. Don't neglect to commit to daily study of the word of God so that you can embrace his grace and mercy.

Love covers a multitude of sins. Anyone who has mishandled you must repay their debt. Remember to make eviction of bitterness a repetitive action and seek forgiveness until it takes up residence in your heart.

Expedient timing is what we can expect when the father steps in for his child(ren). His timing is impeccable regardless of how impatient we are with Him.

Never will God give up on us so we can never give up on Him. There is a song that says *"God can do just what He said He would do, and He will fulfill every desire in you."* Remember who your redeemer is.

It was the day of my mother's failed suicide attempt that the key was thrown into the abyss of darkness never to be found. That key would unlock my freedom into adulthood to allow me to be a well-rounded individual able to develop and maintain healthy relationships with those around me, yet Satan had other plans.

I vowed that day that I would never allow anything in my life to get me down so bad that I would consider taking my own life. I tried diligently to feel okay. I tried to feel normal but, in some way, nothing was normal about me. At this point, Satan stood beside me and reminded me that I was unwanted by my mother and since she did not want me, he told me no one else would either. But I had one thing in my favor for people to accept me for me. My body.

Somehow, someway it would all come back to my body being used for the satisfaction of others. To gain and maintain control, I decided to give it to whomever I chose at my leisure so no one would have to take it again against my will or desire.

When you look back over your life, can you think of things that you may have done due to trying to protect your inner child?

Take a moment to reflect over your life and write out the things you may have done to protect your inner child and use the lines below to journal about it.

Chapter 4

A Little Girl's Secret

Through everything that happened over the course of my childhood and into my early teens, much of it was a blur because I wanted to forget about so many things. As I stated earlier, you can stuff a lot of things when it plays on your mental health and you are fighting to not feel like you are losing your mind.

As a little girl I always felt close to God and believed He could help me with anything except my one secret. I could not tell anyone this secret because I was afraid that if I did, my friends and family would not like me. I can remember being around eight years old and spending a lot of time in my room playing with my dolls and stuffed animals.

They were my friends who knew how to keep secrets. I would masturbate and then tell my "friends" how good it felt and wished they could share the same experience with me. My belief was that my mother knew what I was doing but never said anything to me about it but another part of me was not for sure.

As I reflect over my life, there is a part of me that wished she had caught me and asked why, or who I had learned this behavior from but, it was a conversation that never took place. As I ponder it, I realize on so many levels why it never did.

First, my mother battled with mental health issues that I believe did not afford her to rationalize the level of parenting that I needed most. Secondly, also what may be most important, is that the events that helped shape me would not have occurred and I would not be penning this book at this very moment.

As I stated earlier, God will take what was stolen from you to get you to your next level if it is intended to bring Glory to Him. A parental lesson I learned through this was to also realize that it is a fundamental problem when as parents we neglect to speak with our children about things early on such as teaching them about good touch, and bad touch.

We cannot ignore the fact that sometimes the violation does not always occur from a stranger. Oftentimes it is through someone you know, trust, and potentially love. When we overlook these conversations, it leads to failing to see the issues surrounding certain moods and behaviors. Well into adulthood and after getting therapy, I learned that I had suppressed sexual feelings and it was never addressed in a healthy way.

Early in childhood I stumbled across masturbation and overtime the need to provide self-satisfaction became a bad habit. I do not know where I learned it from but eventually it led to promiscuity.

Promiscuity was a behavior I embarked upon at an early age because I thought this was the answer to my problem. Remember earlier I told you that myself and my childhood friend had experienced similar situations with molestation.

Through conversation, we found out we both had the same desires and formed a relationship that would go from just being friends to two people who would satisfy one another's sexual desires because no one else would in the capacity that we wanted.

Do you see the sick sorted method in which Satan works to deceive you into believing wrong is right? We were kids talking about sexual desires and what felt good to us and going on sexual exploits with one another.

For me it was fulfilling multiple desires because keep in mind, I also had feelings of being unloved, unwanted, and worthless to which I also later learned stemmed from what is known as unresolved abandonment issues.

I understand now that my battle with these feelings was because it just so happened, I was an unwanted pregnancy. I told you earlier, my mother got involved with a man who was *supposedly* separated from his wife and ended up pregnant with me.

Because she was already a single parent with one child and still living at home with her mother, she did not want to bring another child into this world without a father. Some people are not aware that an unwanted/unplanned pregnancy can be open portals for children to battle with spirits of abandonment and rejection.

In Susan Anderson's *"The Journey from Abandonment to Healing"* she explains how unresolved abandonment can also lead to other ailments such as anxiety, obsessive and compulsive behaviors, and low self-esteem.

Because of the sexual molestation coupled with the abandonment and rejection, it was a perfect combination for Satan to strip me of my personal identity leaving me confused about who I truly was in Christ.

By the time I reached puberty, I had no interest in boys in the sense of having a boyfriend. I was more interested in chasing sexual desires however, I had also been introduced to Christ as my personal Savior by now and I wanted to please Him so I would not go to hell.

Afterall, I had been reading the Bible for years now and I understood that sinners would be thrown into a lake of fire to burn forever, and I did not find that very inviting. This issue that I battled with would certainly send me to hell without a doubt.

Because of low self-esteem, I was charmed into believing that the "high" I was chasing could only be obtained with a specific individual. Little did I know that charm would get me wrapped up into a deceitful entanglement that would make me feel like that scum of the earth.

If you've never believed in the saying, "If it sounds too good to be true, it usually is," BELIEVE IT. Satan does not give us anything without there being strings attached. If you remember that it will prevent you from doing a lot of things that might go against your better judgement.

Over time, I was manipulated, or might I say, I agreed to the manipulation of befriending someone to cover up the mess that was going on between the two of us. It was no longer about a mutual relationship amongst two friends, it became the most deceitful of human behavior that I could ever imagine myself to be entangled with. Mixed with lust, lasciviousness, and deception, I was trapped in my own mental jail not knowing how to break free. Thankfully with time and maturity along with God's grace and mercy, we are still alive, and eventually I was able to walk away and be able to reconcile my wrongs and repent for my actions.

The lady I violated for the sake of sex, later became one of my closest friends I have known as well as a true Sister in Christ. I am a living testimony of the words Joseph spoke to his brothers in Genesis.

What Satan meant for evil; God turned that situation into good. As a matter of fact, at the 2nd Annual SMAC Talk Huddle, my sister-friend, Yolanda, and I shared love, hugs, laughter, tears, and more importantly the mess that turned into a message.

Our mess became a message that was able to empower other women on how to authentically affirm, confirm, mold, and motivate one another. This is what solidified the SMAC Talk brand where SMAC stands for sisters, mothers, aunts, and cousins. The mission is to affirm, confirm, mold, and motivate others to be all they were created to be. Be on the lookout for information about the next Annual Huddle by following me on Facebook @MrsAnnBey.

Being stripped of self-awareness leaves you feeling naked and vulnerable if you are sensitive to the chaos that happens in life. For some, you may not have a heightened awareness of it. Once you start to view life and its circumstances from a lens in which you have always viewed it, the picture becomes clearer, and you realize that something must change. I would like you to think about your own life and earnestly ask yourself the following questions and then journal your answers.

Has anyone ever coerced you to believing a lie for the sake of getting what they want from you? How did it make you feel?

Use the journal lines below to uncover your deceiver's actions in your life. In doing so, you will feel a sense of empowerment knowing the enemy has been exposed!

_____

_____

_____

_____

_____

_____

_____

_____

_____

_____

_____

_____

_____

_____

Chapter 5

Mental Poverty

I am quite sure you are probably wondering what mental poverty is right? Well, we understand what the meaning of mental and poverty is correct? Well perhaps some may not so I will define these terms for you. According to Merriam-Webster the terms are defined as follows:

> Mental- a). of or relating to the mind b). of or relating to intellectuals as contrasted with emotional activity [mental acuity] c). of, relating to, or being intellectual as contrasted with overt physical activity d). occurring or experienced in the mind and lastly e). relating to the mind, its activity, or its products as an object of study f). relating to spirit or idea as opposed to matter.

For the point I'm making, I want you to focus on item b. which relates to mental acuity or sharpness of intellect as well as emotional activity.

> Poverty- a). the state of being poor
>   b). a lack of something.

I want you to focus on the latter of the two definitions of poverty and when we placed the two words together considering the definitions I have pointed out, we can see that mental poverty simply means lacking in mental acuity as it relates to intellectual and emotional sharpness.

What does that all mean? It simply means that when Satan robs you of your spiritual identity, your mental acuity is also damaged. You can liken your heart to the glass windows a thief may break to gain entry to a home he is in pursuit of robbing, a lock that has been picked for the thief breaking into a safe.

At a point into my younger adulthood, I struggled with not wanting to be like my mother and going in and out of a mental hospital battling with depression, experiencing several failed relationships, and not being able to provide the mental, spiritual, and emotional support my children needed.

Let me tell you, the struggle was real and by the time I was thirty-four years old, I felt like a failure because I was in the midst of a mentally and emotionally abusive marriage that I was desperately trying to hold together all while lacking the proper tools to do so with no outside support from anyone I felt I could trust to talk to about it.

I want to pause here and tell anyone who may be going through a troubling relationship, get proper help and please do not try and force a relationship to work. It takes two people that are willing to work together and the work is not from one person's viewpoint, it takes both parties having input on what it will take to make the relationship work.

Now although that is another book, I wanted to put that into the atmosphere because there are a lot of, both women and men, out there that are suffering in silence because they feel they are alone in their marital or relational journey. I have been there, and I know how emotionally draining it is. I also know how influential it is to your mental wellbeing.

For me, I was afraid that if I walked away, he would be right about me being a *"Piss poor excuse for a mother and wife"* My thoughts became; Of course! This was the reason I had battled all the years with the negative emotions I felt for so long and finally I had someone come along and put an identification on it. It was hereditary.

I was just like my mom and grandma. It had to be true because my husband of five years and counting had said it. Little did either of us know and realize Satan was utilizing him as part of the plan to cause me to go deeper into mental poverty. One thing we must realize is that we all have a Judas in our life, and we cannot get caught up on who God uses more so than understanding why He is using them. I can tell you this and you can stand on it without a doubt. People honestly do serve in our lives for a reason, a season, and then there are the ones that are there for a lifetime.

It behooves us to find out the difference so that we are not holding on to relationships that God is trying to remove us from. Anyway, back to what I was saying.

Satan has a plan and purpose for our lives just as God does. We simply must be in alignment with whose plan and purpose we are going to walk by. Unfortunately, we are sometimes too spiritually malnourished and weak to fight the spiritual battle that we end up in the ring getting spanked until God steps in and says *"No more. Satan take your hands off my child!"* I was in the battle for sure, but I was not fighting much. I got to a point where I lost my desire to fight. I contemplated thoughts of suicide because it seemed like the easiest thing to do. I fought with the thought many times, but the thing that kept my consciousness clear were my babies.

I could not have the trauma I experienced to be their story too. I remembered that day over and over watching her pills hit the floor. I remembered when I didn't want to remember and what Satan kept playing to me was that my mother felt more okay to leave me than to stay and take care of me because she loved me that much.

I want to point out also that mental poverty will cause some people to perform self-injurious behaviors to try and cope with the pain they feel inside. However, I would like to suggest to anyone reading this right now that if you know someone, or you yourself feel like the only way to resolve your internal emotions is cause self-harm by cutting, swallowing, using substances, or putting oneself at risk with having unprotected or dangerous sexual encounters, contact your local hospital, seek therapy, speak with a licensed counselor, reach out to a pastor or as a last result contact a trusted family member or friend.

Believe me that the struggles become greater because Satan's goal is to keep you from reaching your God given destiny and for him to do that, he has to keep your mind clouded by negative judgement and present fear tactics that if you reach out for help, people will judge and think less of you. Let me encourage you today: God always sees the best in you because you are fearfully and wonderfully made according to Psalms 139:14.

When you review the past few years of your life, can you compare where you were mentally, emotionally, and physically? Were you in a good place then and how does it compare to now?

These are some in depth questions you can ask yourself at any point in your life but for the sake of looking at mental poverty, I want you to journal the following question.

What lies have been spoken to you by Satan through a friend or loved one?

_____

_____

_____

_____

_____

_____

_____

_____

_____

_____

_____

_____

_____

_____

_____

_____

Now that you have written out the things that have been spoken to or about you, say this prayer:

"Dear Lord, I forgive the people that have spoken ill against me as well as to me. I break every word curse that has ever been spoken over my life in the name of Jesus and I declare that I am everything you have created me to be, and I will continue to seek and walk out the plan and purpose you have for my life by the power of the Blood of Jesus Christ, Amen!"

Identify

Disable

Exterminate

Never

Trust

Ignore

Thank

Yield

Chapter 6

Releasing the Victim Spirit

So many people in the world today carry a spirit of victimization and do not know it. Victimization is defined by Merriam Webster as *to make a victim of.* Clearly that does not sound like something inflicted upon us by God, does it?

When it comes to stealing your identity, Satan often uses what appears to be real to get you to buy into the lie. In the world of psychology, victimization is defined as an act or process of singling out someone for cruel or unfair treatment, typically through physical or emotional abuse.

Was I victimized with intent, ill intent, or by happenstance? I cannot say that my perpetrators violated me on purpose because I know and understand now that Satan had his plan devised all along from the beginning of my existence.

I understand that he didn't want this story to be told because it might give another individual hope and encouragement to discover or rebuild their own spiritual identity. I did not see it from a position of victimization at the time and had I chosen to verbally share things I was going through at that time, had someone accused me of behaving like a victim, I would have totally disagreed.

However, because of my embarrassment, I didn't talk about my life in many details. I did not want there to be questions that I might have to answer. This my love is victimization. All that I was experiencing made me a victim of my circumstance. You see, we can be victims in our own mind and even cause ourselves to become physically ill depending on how deep the matter is.

Overcoming the spirit of victimization is easier said than done for some. It seems to be more common, and people tend to wear the behavior as if it is an article of clothing, putting it on when it is convenient for the sake of gaining empathy from those around them and then placing it on a shelf when they are no longer in need of it.

I'm making this point because as we are talking about rebuilding spiritual identity and looking at how Satan robs us of our identity, we must remember that when we walk around with the spirit of victimization on our shoulders, we weaken our faith in God as well as dilute our testimony of God being our Jehovah Jireh, Jehovah Rapha, Jehovah Shalom and more.

My life coach, who is also an International Best-Selling Author, penned a book titled *Beloved:*

Experiencing God and Abba in a Fatherless Generation (p75). I was sitting there, speed reading as I normally do before I read a book and this specific sentence leaped off the page at me. I affixed my eyes on this sentence and had to repeat it over and over, *"God, who am I"*?

Sometimes, to discover your personal identity, you must ask God, who am I? And then, what does this have to do with victimization? When you look at some of the reasons why you might carry this spirit, such as for myself, you find that it is because of the people that you put your trust in; not thinking about the fact that people will let you down. But remember, God never will.

One might find it easy to blame everyone close to them for everything bad that happens in life, however, it is not always conducive for personal growth. It's not enough to recognize when you have been the victim of misconduct, but overcoming is a direct responsibility of each individual and may take time so don't get impatient if you attempt to forgive someone, but the feelings keep resurfacing.

You must simply continue to declare and release the words of forgiveness into the situation until the words reach from your mouth to your heart.

Releasing the victimization spirit may also require you to open your mind and heart up to deal with your past trauma by forgiving someone who has violated you, and you might even have to forgive yourself.

For the release to be effective it will be imperative for you to acknowledge where you are mentally, emotionally, and spiritually as these are all components that make up your personal identity and to rebuild it, we must recognize which entities are most affected.

I want to pause right here and provide you with this mindset renovation tool known as the IDENTITY Identifier. The purpose of this tool is to help you cultivate a mindset for finding, building, or getting to know your identity based on where you are in life at this moment.

Later, I am also going to give you an additional resource called Hidden Treasures which is a 7-Day Personal Discovery Journal that is designed to further assist you with discovering your Hidden Treasures.

These tools combined with the resources I am linking at the end of the book are going to place you well on your pathway to taking back what the enemy has stolen from you.

Identify what the primary cause of your lack may be. Are there decisions that need to be made that may affect a needed change and does that change begin with me?

Disable the enemy's power by obtaining the necessary tools that will equip you to walk out your life assignment. Keep in mind we may not all be preachers or evangelists, but we each have an assignment that we must complete.

Exterminate the negative mindset that continues to keep you bound by limiting belief systems. Seek counseling by a professional if needed and don't allow bad counsel to discourage you from doing so. Remember misery loves company and gets a real kick out of a party crew.

Never give up on dreams and desires that are within your heart of hearts. Don't allow external factors to impact your internal gauges that constantly remind you that you were created for greater things than what's right in front of you.

Trust the process that you must walk through. Some of the most precious of jewels are created under extreme pressure.

<u>Ignore</u> the negative Nancy's in life who always have a word of advice but seldom have words of encouragement when they see you on your journey. The people who utterly understand your walk will be there to genuinely support and/or pray you through.

<u>Thank</u> God for everything regardless of what it looks like. Remember your attitude will always determine your altitude therefore the more negatively you speak, the less momentum you will be able to obtain to get the wind beneath your wings so that you can soar.

<u>Yield</u> to the Holy Spirit and allow God to lead you wherever He has for you to go, and do not be afraid. Know that He has gone before you and made your journey possible.

Chapter 7

Disbelief + Doubt = Unbelief

Have you ever been so disgruntled with how things are going in life until you are in a state of disbelief that things could even be going the way that they are?

More importantly, you are in disbelief that it is happening to you. You wonder what you may have done so horribly to deserve the black carpet that was laid out in life for you to walk down.

Well, that is me. I could not believe just how awful life had been presented to me. It started with the belief that my mother did not want me so I resolved that no one else would want me ever.

That faulty thinking produced what is known as a subconscious lie that is normally transmitted during the formative years of life (*The Lies That Bind*).

When these subconscious lies are developing, unless there is someone there to help a child to reverse the lies or assist with cognitive restructuring as the child grows, you end up as an adult with years of a false sense of personal views that needs cognitive restructuring and resocialization therapy.

The other option is to maneuver relationships in a dysfunctional manner such as the way I did. My method of dealing with the subconscious lie was to make it a point to sever relationships before they had an opportunity to evolve into anything authentic.

By early adulthood I had already concluded that God either hated me, or He was not real because there was no way I could experience life as it was, handed down by a loving and caring Father.

Eventually doubt would begin to creep into my mind and quite honestly, I started doubting His existence. This made me fearful because I wanted so desperately to believe that I was tripping.

However, I was extremely doubtful that the loving and caring Father that I so adored and wanted to please from the time I was a little girl existed. My children were getting older and did not have a stable environment. They did not have stable parents or stable adults around them to provide them the guidance and support they needed. I would spend a great deal praying that someone, anyone would give me a magical answer to make the pain go away or at least stop it for a while.

I knew that life was not always going to be great, but I prayed that life would at least be good to me for a minute.

Hmph, isn't it funny how when you feel like your back is against the wall, somewhere in the midst of your chaotic thinking, you are either self-sabotaging in life or depending on where you are or were on your spiritual journey, you are whispering those silent prayers begging God to throw you a lifeline because what you are really doing is testing Him?

Hopefully, there are more of the silent prayers than the self-sabotaging behaviors because God is listening for our cries and our angels are waiting to be dispatched on our behalf.

My negative thoughts went on for years to the point that I began to abuse cold and flu medicine to numb the pain that I was feeling from having to get up and deal with life daily.

This went on for at least one and a half years. My disbelief and doubt eventually led me to develop an unbelieving mindset. Notice I said mindset. We must understand that sin starts in our mind primarily, not the heart.

I am so thankful God had my heart guarded and did not let the stinking thinking enter my heart. God only knows where I would be today had that been the case.

I had honestly begun to doubt the existence of God as the creator of heaven and earth, good and evil. I could only see Him as a God who allowed a woman, wife, and mother to go through hell and high water with no intended outcome.

At the time I could not fully see the picture that had been painted in 1971, before I was formed in my mother's womb. No one could have paid me to see how the scripture, Jeremiah 29:11 could relate to me too, so I certainly did not believe that he had a plan and purpose for me. I only saw the plan that was meant to hurt me and break me down to the lowest common denominator of human life.

I just wanted to die but He would not allow me to entertain the thought for long. I would have periods of momentary peace in my mind and heart that things were going to get better soon and suddenly out of nowhere, the tsunami would roll in again.

It was called hope. He gave me just enough hope to keep me coming back to Him every time; God that is.

Eventually I had had enough and cried out to Him in anger asking why He continued to allow things to transpire the way they did. He had shown me success and given me a taste of His goodness.

Why couldn't I sustain it? God will give you a taste of what He has in store for you. However, you must put your full trust in Him and not waver from His truths.

Additionally, you must be able to manage it and because He loves us enough to not give us things prematurely, He will withhold certain gifts from us until we are responsible enough to oversee what He has for us.

Think about what I just shared then ask yourself, how have you doubted God as it relates to His promises? Has He promised you something and it seems like it will never happen?

Take a moment to journal your answers below and be transparent with yourself.

Chapter 8

My Pain Paved the Way

When I reflect over my life now, I understand better how Satan utilized my life's experiences to attempt to shape my identity into who he wanted me to be versus who God identifies me as.

Some situations presented to me in life could have led me to suffer from more serious mental health issues. However, due to the environment I grew up in, it served as a shield of protection because I was always aware and conscious of my thoughts.

I had vowed as a little girl that I would never allow things to get to me as badly as they had my mother, the day she attempted to take her own life. There were times I carelessly put my shield down to go and play in areas of life I should not have.

Satan would like to have taken my shield away forever, but my guardian angel was always there to wrestle it away from him so that I would have a means of protecting my spiritual identity even when I did not realize what the shield was for.

Because of brokenness, I severed many relationships. I had a misconception that people would leave me before there was a behavior or situation to warrant the action. I fought to hold on to relationships that were not meant to be lifetime relationships but let go of others out of ignorance because I felt I wasn't good enough to be in the company of certain individuals.

It was easy to not set myself up for disappointment, I thought. I later found out this behavior is known as imposter syndrome. It is defined as working hard to get others to like you, yet feeling like you are not worthy of being in their presence.

To this day, I am still conditioning my mind to walk in the affirmation that *"I am good enough,* and that *"I deserve to be in every room I enter."*

Does that surprise you when I say that? Well, even as I write this out, I know that I am not where I desire to be, but surely, I am not where I use to be and if I can overcome identity theft, SO CAN YOU!

So how does one get the courage to move forward, you might be asking. Truthfully, you may never get the courage to move forward. I would be lying if I told you, it was something I have the courage to do. What *did* happen to me was that I had an urge and strong enough desire within my gut to walk the path to finding out what the feeling was all about that I experienced that day while sitting in my office.

I knew something felt familiar with the things I daydreamed about while growing up. My dreams of helping people heal through difficult phases of life never left me, they were just embedded deep within, hidden by layers of life's circumstances that prevented my true identity from being recognized whenever I looked at myself in a mirror.

I believed caring for my mother equipped me to have that kind of passion for other people, but Satan had plans to strip me of that.

I had experienced enough pain in my life and began to see where it stemmed from. Some was a result of self-sabotaging behaviors, and some of it was direct afflictions that I had to endure to build in me the strong, independent, and resilient individual that I am today.

In the words of my dear friend and little sister Michelle, my pain has finally paid. It paved the way for me to reach out to others to affirm, confirm, mold, and motivate others to be all they were created to be. I feel very strongly about the fact that no one should have to build or rebuild on their own.

It requires reliance on walking through the Word of God to understand his love for you, the extension of His love through other people, and His expert counsel in the form of therapists whose reliance is on the wisdom of God.

In reclaiming my victory, I have learned a lot about myself along the journey and though it has not been easy, it has been rewarding. When you've come to the realization that Satan has committed identity theft against you, I want to encourage you to press into God. Reclaiming your victory begins and ends with you, all you have to do now is continue the work.

What Didn't Kill Me
Antoinette J Bey

Screams, yells, cries, and lies to mask the pain I feel inside. I cover my eyes and my ears because I don't want to see anymore or hear any more of the chaos that grips my wounded soul. So, I am told that which does not kill us only makes us stronger, but I am no longer strong. You see, I am weak from the weeks turned into years of loneliness turned anger and rage, but Who can I run to, to share this empty space, who can I run to, to burn the page of this horrific chapter of my life? All my life I had to fight. Fight to stay alive, keep my head above the tide. I cannot swim upstream when life keeps washing me down stream. Screams, screaming, yelling, crying, lying to mask the pain I feel inside. My eyes are covered because I don't want to see anymore or hear any more of the chaos that gripped my wounded soul. I was always told that which doesn't kill us would make us stronger and see, I'm stronger now.

Conclusion

Before you go, I want to remind you that your personal identity is your thumbprint in life and cannot be replicated or duplicated. It is original.

When a thief steals a person's identity, they must study the person to try and emulate them as best as they can to pass off as being an original, so technically they are just a carbon copy.

First off, carbon copies of any authentic document, photo, or painting are worth little to nothing which means, anyone attempting to replicate you will not hold or have the same value or weight as you.

Also keep in mind that those who get caught stealing identities get caught because there are some things about a person that cannot be duplicated.

That brings me to this final thought, God does not create carbon copies of us. You are the original of who you are and when Satan comes to try and steal your identity, you must remind him that you are the original and therefore, there is nothing that he can do with your life to make his life any better because when it is all said and done, he is going to hell regardless.

All your giftings and blessings belong to you. Other than you providing him access to your possessions, he cannot take them away. Remember the scripture in Job where he says, the Lord gives, and the Lord takes away (*chapter 1 verse 21*).

Notice that Satan could only take away the things from Job that God allowed. Therefore, his crime against you is an open and shut case. You have the power to charge him with attempting to cloth you with his identity versus the identity God clothed you with when you were in your mother's womb. Satan is guilty of producing a carbon of himself containing fearfulness, rejection, abandonment, brokenness, and insecurities and switching your identity for his.

Your trial of identity theft can become a bit daunting, but I want to make it as easy for you as possible. In addition to using the journal prompts at the end of each chapter as well as the Identity

Identifier in chapter 6, I am also providing you another FREE resource within this book.

As I shared earlier, I have included my 7-Day Personal Discovery Journal to help you continue building upon the work you have already done at the end of the chapter.

I want to help you in uncovering your Hidden Treasures. The prompts are designed to help cultivate a renewed mindset so that you can uncover the Identity Theft and reclaim your victory. When you reach the end of the 7 days, be sure to email me at ann@mrsannbey.com, following the specific instructions at the end of the journal to get another FREE gift from me.

Resources

Beloved: Experiencing God as Abba in a Fatherless Generation- Carla R Cannon

https://www.cde.ca.gov/sp/cd/re/caqdevelopment.asp

dictionary.apa.org/victimization

https://www.healthline.com/health/mental-health/imposter-syndrome

https://www.nctsn.org/sites/default/files/resources/making_the_connection_trauma_substance_abuse.pdf

The Journey from Abandonment to Healing-Susan Anderson

The Lies That Bind: The 100 Most Commonly Seen Unconscious Lies and the Keys to the Locks-Anneshia Freeman, MBA, MSW, CADC-M

7-Day Hidden Treasures Journal-Antoinette J Bey

Hidden Treasures

7 – Day Discovery Journal

This Journal Belongs to:

_____

Hidden Treasures

7 Days to Personal Discovery

Over the next 7 days you will reflect, identify, and reconstruct your thoughts regarding your past by using the guided instructions to fill in the spaces as well as the empty pages for self-reflection. The purpose is to help you discover the HIDDEN TREASURES within you.

~Mrs. Ann

Day One

Many of us have spoken negatively about our own selves or negativity has come from the mouth of others, but today I want you to begin to speak life to the little girl inside of you.

Write down seven affirmations and read them aloud every morning before starting your day and prior to completing your continuing journal exercises.

You can also refer to your affirmations whenever you begin to feel unworthy, discouraged, or just down on yourself, these will serve as a reminder of who you really are on the inside.

These can be what you feel now, or what you desire to become.

I AM

Reflections

Day Two

You know, II Timothy 1:7 says: "For God hath not given us the spirit of fear; but of power, and love, and of a sound mind, so why do we fear? In Psalms 23:4a David said, "Yea, I walk through the valley of the shadow of death, I will fear no evil," and in Psalms 23:6a "Surely goodness and mercy shall follow me".

You may be experiencing tormenting fears because the enemy wants to prevent you from becoming all God wants you to be. My sister, consider this notion; confrontation of your fears is one significant tool to combating and overcoming that fear.

*Date*_____

Write out your fear(s) and once you have your list completed, read them off and after each fear you have listed; declare aloud: <u>For God hath not given</u> **ME** <u>the spirit of fear, but of power, and of love, and of a sound mind!</u>

Reflections

Day Three

Re-sil-ience /rəˈzilyəns/
noun

1. The capacity to recover quickly from difficulties, toughness.
2. The ability of a substance or object to spring back into shape; elasticity.

To live a stress-free life of peace, love, and happiness one must learn to be resilient in the face of adversity. Simply put, you must learn to bounce back from situations that try to keep you bound. Whether it be family problems, relationship problems, financial problems, health problems, or problems within your work environment.

To become resilient, you must define the issues you may be facing. Don't confuse having resiliency with overcoming fears.

And we know that all things work together for good to them who love God, to them who are called according to his purpose.
Romans 8:28

*Date*_____

After reading your affirmations, take five minutes to identify and write out some challenges you may be experiencing as it relates to family, relationships, financial, health & employment.

_____

_____

_____

_____

_____

_____

_____

_____

_____

_____

_____

_____

_____

_____

_____

Reflections

Day Four

Prayerfully you were able to get through day three and not feel like you were ready to throw the journal in the corner of your room while feeling down and gloomy. If you have any negative feelings bubbling up, be sure and direct that energy into your daily journaling. This is important to the momentum of the exercises. Do not cave into the pressure of feeling overwhelmed from looking at yourself from within. I know it can be tough, but it will all be worth it in the end, trust me.

When we can identify different situations that have penetrated our hearts and caused us to develop debilitating mindsets about life, it opens the roadway for reconstruction to begin to take place.

*Date*_____

Take a moment to reflect over your life and think of situations that happened that may have led to you developing an unhealthy mindset related to money, sex, people, etc.

Reflections

Day Five

Today will be a day of refreshing and reflection for you. Take the day to do something nice for yourself such as grabbing a bite to eat and sitting in a park or driving someplace serene to watch the sun set. You can also plan a spa day for yourself. The objective is to spend time alone basking in peace and serenity.

Take your journal with you on your special retreat and jot down your reflective thoughts. Be sure your reflections move you closer to opening your treasure. The objective is to see how far you have come in just a few days.

Date＿＿＿＿＿＿

Reflections

Day Six

If you have made it to Day Six, you may have already experienced slight discomfort but again, I say Sister, hang in there. It will be worth it all in the end.

We have previously looked at some things that may have caused hindrances in our lives and those things are not all-inclusive to what could be staggering our growth process. Now we want to go a little deeper into self-reflection and identify the pain of our past as it relates to childhood.

To help guide this exercise here is a sample of what your entry would look like:

*I became sexually active with a man ten years my senior when I was only 17 years old.

*My uncle molested me between the ages of three and twelve years old.

*Date*_____

For this journal entry, using the examples above, list a minimum of five debilitating truths from any area of your life. (Remember Sister, you cannot confront what you are not willing to come face-to-face with.)

Reflections

Day Seven

Before you go about your day; read your affirmations aloud and then write out the ones that you feel least passionate about at this very moment.

For the one affirmation that you feel least passionate about, write one positive thought to negate the negative thought.

The purpose of this exercise is to help you begin to see the importance of reconstructing the mindset. Here is an example of what your entry would look like.

e.g. I Am Sexy [affirmation] {but} My butt and thighs are too big [least passionate due to my difficult weight loss journey], {however}, My husband loves me as I am.

*Date*_____

What affirmation do I feel less positive/passionate about?
Why? Write one positive thought to negate
the negative thought.

Reflections

As we work through unmasking and uncovering some of our gems, we discover we have an entire treasure chest of valuable merchandise. That merchandise equates to our talents, our gifts, our desire, passions, dreams, goals, aspirations, and abilities.

After the seventh day of your journaling process, you should be able to identify things that will require more of your attention. With a careful and in-depth analysis of your entries, jot down at least three key areas of your life that you would like to focus more attention on.

These are the areas of my life
I would like to give more focus to:

Hidden Treasures was originally written as a standalone tool for those who were unsure if coaching was something they were ready for, yet they wanted to delve into a useful self-help tool that they could use to process and help break down debilitating thoughts that hinder one from achieving their next best. I hope you have found these additional journal prompts beneficial.

I have shared with you the raw and uncut version of the path it took to rebuild my own spiritual identity as well as given you some tools and this additional resource to help you get on the road to repairing your own. I would love to hear from you.

Additionally, if you have issues that stem from childhood trauma or, from a previous toxic relationship that has caused you to struggle with:

❖ *low self-esteem*
❖ *abuse*
❖ *addiction*
❖ *codependency*
❖ *self-sabotaging behaviors*
❖ *unconscious beliefs*

I would love to speak with you to see if we can work together to help walk you through overcoming obstacles that may be causing stagnation or hindrances in your personal life. Email me today at ann@mrsannbey.com and include three things that most resonated with you in the book as well as three key areas of your life you would like to give more focus to. Be sure to include items requested.

*Following the instructions will allow you to receive a **FREE** 25 minute consultation with me. I look forward to meeting you soon to help you finish discovering those Hidden Treasures!*

❖ Please note: Failure to complete the instructions correctly will disqualify you from this FREE consultation

About the Author

Antoinette J Bey is a wife, mother, daughter, and voice of reason to many. She is a Trailblazers University Certified Life Coach, Author, and the Visionary of SMAC Talk w/ Mrs. Ann. One of her greatest desires is to see women (and men) healed, whole, and set free so that they can live to become all they were created to be. She holds an Associate's in Interdisciplinary studies as well as a Bachelor's in Psychology from Liberty University with a concentration in Addiction and Recovery and Christian Counseling.

Antoinette understands what it is like to struggle with issues of the heart internally while lacking a community of people who genuinely care about the direction, or the (re)construction of your life.

In her latest book, Identity Theft she encourages readers to know that they are not alone on this path of life and this resource serves as a useful tool to help you jumpstart your journey to revealing and healing from spiritual identity theft in your personal life.

Contact

Email:
ann@mrsannbey.com

Website:
http://www.mrsannbey.com/

NOTES:

NOTES:

NOTES:

Made in the USA
Monee, IL
28 February 2022

91734432R00066